To:

_____

From:

_____

_____

Prayers
for My Baby Girl

HARVEST HOUSE PUBLISHERS
EUGENE, OREGON

written by
Angela Thomas

photography by
Julie Johnson

Prayers for My Baby Girl
Text Copyright © 2011 by Angela Thomas
Photography © Julie Johnson, Vine Images

Published by Harvest House Publishers
Eugene, Oregon 97402
www.harvesthousepublishers.com

ISBN 978-0-7369-3937-9

Design and production by Koechel Peterson and Associates, Minneapolis, Minnesota
Material adapted from *Prayers for Mothers of Newborns* by Angela Thomas, copyright © 2000, 2004

Printed in China

12 13 14 15 16 17 18 / LP / 10 9 8 7 6 5

For Taylor and AnnaGrace

It is a joy to pray
for my baby girls
who will become
beautiful women of God.

The Gift

Oh, wonderful Lord,

Today we brought home our gift. Awesome. Breathtaking. Stunning. Surely, she is the most amazing gift I have ever known. It is love at first sight, and I am consumed with pride. I am totally at peace. Finally, the one we have prayed for has safely arrived and come home.

The whole day has been dreamlike. A tiny new outfit just for the ride home. A proud daddy with a complicated car seat. Video and pictures and good-byes to the nurses. A car full of balloons, the first breeze through her hair, and her first ride in a minivan. Our joy in introducing her to the whole family.

Now there is a new life in our home. Someone lies in the cradle, sleeping as if she has always been here. She breathes and squirms as if she's done it for years. We find great delight in just watching her sleep. Blankets and diapers are now scattered throughout the house. Dirty baby clothes already need washing. This sleeping little bundle has quickly established her place in our home and our hearts.

Thank You, God, for answering our prayers. Thank You for this homecoming. Thank You for the gift of our child. I can look into the eyes of our gift and see my own reflection. I am so humbled. I never could have dreamed what this day would be like. I am a mother, she is my child, and we are home.

I bless You, God. I am happy and full of Your favor. Truly, You are an awesome God. In Jesus' name, I pray. Amen.

Behold, children are a gift of the Lord,
The fruit of the womb is a reward.

—Psalm 127:3 NASB

Wonderfully Made

O GOD,

This child You gave us is already so precious to me. She is Your creation, fearfully and wonderfully made. You deserve all my praise. I hold her against my tummy and cannot believe she came from me. Although I tried, I could not imagine the magnificent work You were doing in the secret place of my womb.

Her skin is the softest I have ever touched— her fingers and toes, perfection. Her full head of hair swirls in a silly and wayward fashion. It must be pure silk just spun by an angel. Her big eyes with great eyelashes, her little bird mouth, her tightly clenched fists—I am intrigued by every part of her. Even the smell of her newness thrills me. I could linger forever at the nape of her neck, praying that I

will never forget her fresh fragrance. I am awestruck by Your creation. I want to shout from the highest place, in my loudest voice, "My God is almighty; my God is miraculous." I hold her tightly, and I sing. I sing hymns. I sing lullabies. I just sing. I praise You for this child who has come and filled a place in my heart—a mommy place that was there all along and waiting for her.

I feel keenly aware that my life will never be the same. Yet I wouldn't go back for all the treasure in the world. How did I ever live without her? Thank You, sweet Lord, for the immeasurable gift of our baby. "Your works are wonderful, I know that full well." Hallelujah. Amen.

For you created my inmost being;
   you knit me together in my mother's womb.
I praise you because I am fearfully and wonderfully made;
   your works are wonderful,
   I know that full well.
My frame was not hidden from you
   when I was made in the secret place.
When I was woven together in the depths of the earth,
your eyes saw my unformed body.

—Psalm 139:13~16

Pure Love

The ability to fully embrace the verses of 1 Corinthians 13—the love chapter—has always eluded me. To purely apply it to my life seemed impossible and beyond my capacity...until now. For me, to love my baby is to begin to know pure love. Only through her am I coming to understand the depth of Your love for me.

I have come to possess a patience I never thought possible. Its origin must certainly be this well of pure love that has been filled by the birth of my baby. I never knew the depth of comfort I could give until my own was sick. I never thought I could truly love someone else more than myself. But when love is pure, it comes so easily.

To have a child, and then remember that You love me as Your child, gives me new insight. Now I know why You say You will never stop loving me. How could any good mother stop loving her child? I see why You intervene to discipline and protect. What decent parent wouldn't do the same? I feel more secure about Your promises for my future. Just like a child, I trust in Your provision, my providing Parent.

I commit my unending love to my baby. With Your help and through Your fathomless love, I will do my best to always protect, always trust, always hope, and always preserve. May my love for her never fail. May I extend to her the pure and eternal love that only You can give. Amen.

Love is patient, love is kind. It does not envy, it does not boast, it is not proud. It does not dishonor others, it is not self-seeking, it is not easily angered, it keeps no record of wrongs. Love does not delight in evil but rejoices with the truth. It always protects, always trusts, always hopes, always perseveres. Love never fails.

—1 Corinthians 13:4-8

Shared Joy

FATHER GOD,

A wonderful part of our "baby blessing" is found in sharing this abundant joy with friends and relatives. What fun I had designing a birth announcement, introducing her to the world, and proclaiming our delight and gratitude. With each address, I imagined our friends joining us in the celebration of her birth. The birth of our child creates a great reason for rejoicing.

The many cards and gifts bring sweet blessings as each one expresses heartfelt acknowledgment of shared joy. And the joy continues every time someone peeks into her car seat or asks to hold her. I am very proud. With great delight, I share her.

Do You too share in all the excitement? I know that You do! I imagine that You smile like a proud father at every birth. It must thrill You to introduce each of Your new and precious creations...to watch parents experience the most phenomenal event on earth...to witness the unbelievable power of love. Surely, the birth of each baby is Your personalized proclamation of extravagant love and commitment to us all.

Lord, thank You for the joy You have given us to share. She is amazing. You are so generous to entrust her to us. We will continue to share her with others and remind them that she is a gift from Your gracious hand. From my heart of joy, I find it a pleasure to pray. Amen.

When it was time for Elizabeth to have her baby, she gave birth to a son. Her neighbors and relatives heard that the Lord had shown her great mercy, and they shared her joy.

—*Luke* 1:57~58

Heaven Eyes

My dear God in heaven,

What a delight and a mystery it is to watch our baby girl. Seemingly too young to respond, in her sleep she can smile the grandest smiles and even laugh aloud. She will stare at the ceiling as if intently watching something. I wonder what she sees. I wonder what causes her laughter. I wonder if she still sees through "heaven eyes." Can she still glimpse the angels who came with her from heaven? Do they make her laugh out loud? Do they sing her to sleep? Do they make her smile while she dreams?

I know that You assign angels to watch over her. I am very grateful. Thank You for supernatural supervision. I find comfort in knowing that heavenly defenders protect my precious treasure. You appoint guardian angels and give them direct access to Yourself. How much You must care for little children.

I cannot envision an angel, but I believe. I cannot comprehend Your greatness, but I believe. I cannot understand the mysteries of heaven, but I believe. I believe that You love me. I believe that You are the Master Creator and a compassionate God.

I would love to have "heaven eyes" in order to behold Your supernatural work. But by faith, until the day when I have new eyes, I will believe that there is so much more than I can see.

Thank You for all that You do, both seen and unseen, to care for me and my family. Thank You for angels that come and protect babies and make them smile. By faith, I pray by all the power that is in heaven. Amen.

See that you do not despise one of these little ones. For I tell you that their angels in heaven always see the face of my Father in heaven.

—Matthew 18:10

Come Look at Her

Dear God of great joy,

Even at two in the morning, I don't really mind the cries and feedings. I truly delight in just one more look. I cannot get enough. I love to stand and stare at her. I love to see her sleep. I adore her yawn. I watch as her eyes follow the mobile, and I am happy. I work around the house for a few minutes and then give in to the urge to go peek at her again. With every glimpse of her perfect face, I breathe a prayer of thanksgiving. My soul rejoices over her.

Her half smile and inquisitive stare entrance me. I call everyone to come and look at her when she is wide awake and curious. Thankfully, our whole family loves to marvel at this gift who breathes and sleeps and eats. I want my heart to memorize each one of these moments, things not captured by video or camera—her touch, her smell, the emotion that consumes me when I look at her.

O God, I continue to rejoice in the birth of our daughter. My days may be long and extremely tiring, but just one more look can revive my joy. I feel so grateful to You for the wonder of her. I never imagined the breathtaking beauty of motherhood. What a fabulous view! The most spectacular place on earth must surely be our nursery with the priceless treasure sleeping there.

Thank You so much for the privilege of parenting. Thank You for each tender look that warms my heart. My greatest blessing is motherhood. I love You. In Your great name, I pray. Amen.

May your father and mother rejoice;
may she who gave you birth be joyful!

—*Proverbs 23:25*

A woman giving birth to a child
has pain because her time
has come; but when her baby is
born she forgets the anguish
because of her joy that a child
is born into the world.

—John 16:21

First Smile

Jesus,

My world stood joyously still today. I peeked in on the baby, and she smiled at me. No, it wasn't just gas. There was no mistaking it. This was no fluke or a quirky little smile. She looked thrilled to see me. Her whole face brightened. Her arms waved and her feet got happy. Her eyes sparkled. She tried to make gurgling noises. She did everything her little body could do to tell me that she loves me.

Wow! I cannot formulate words to completely describe the condition of my heart. Abundantly full. Content. Wildly happy. Moved. Her smile exhilarates. She inspires me to be a great mama. I am bursting with every motherly emotion. Compassion. Tenderness. Protection. Devotion.

There is truth in Your words. A mother does forget her pain as she comes to know the great joy of her child. I would gladly do every miserable day all over again. Love is such a mighty thing. Love captivates and surprises me. I never dreamed that I had the capacity to love so purely.

Lord, thank You for the smile that has made me stronger. My resolve increases. I want to learn how to love my daughter well. I commit to treat her delicate little spirit with great respect. These are the tender years when character develops. Let me gently care for the heart and mind on the other side of her smile.

Does it move You when we look up and see You and rejoice in Your presence? Oh, Lord, I hope You are pleased by my love and deep admiration for You. I pray that my life will show You that I love You. Amen.

She'll Call Me Mommy

Dear Father, my guide,

I walk into the room, and my daughter jumps with great excitement. Her eyes dance, and her feet kick. She watches my every move with tremendous delight. I look into her bright eyes and realize that I am the one she'll be watching for a very long time. I am the one who will teach her how to act like a lady, I am the one who will model godliness and grace.

When I call her name, she turns her head to remind me that I am the one she will listen to. She will learn about caring and attitude and love from the inflection of my tones and from the choice of my words. She will laugh a little like me and cry about the things that make me cry. Then one day she'll say to herself, "I cannot believe it; I sound just like my mother."

In my mind, I imagine the person I want her to see when she watches me. That person is a God-fearing woman, tender and strong. A woman who laughs easily. A woman who loves endlessly. A woman I am still striving to be. I know that my child watches me, Lord. She makes me want to be that woman even more.

The responsibility is great, and the years are few. I fall on Your mercy and ask for divine intervention and assistance. For the sake of my child, let me be a mother whom she can call "blessed." Because little eyes see and little ears hear, I commit to continue praying and growing. In Jesus, I am able. Amen.

Her children arise and call her blessed.
—Proverbs 31:28

In a Blink

Oh, Lord,

She grows so fast! It seems like we just brought her home from the hospital yesterday. Now she is rolling all over the floor. She holds her head up high to survey the world. She can reach for anything and eventually find a way to get it into her mouth. She's just about to outgrow the infant carrier. We skipped right past the nine-month-sized clothing. Where have the days gone?

When I was a child, time seemed to drag by so slowly. I remember thinking the fourth grade was the longest year of my life. It felt like I wore a size 6X forever. Birthdays took a whole lifetime to come again. Christmas arrived even slower. The days seemed longer, because there was only me to think about and few responsibilities.

Now the days sail by. There is so much to do. The little sweetie who used to sleep all the time now needs one and a half naps a day. The baby who once sat and leisurely watched the world go by now wants—no, demands—some interaction. I feel like I turned around twice, and my newborn became an infant.

In a blink, she'll be grown. It rips my heart out to think about it. Lord, if there's any way I can hold these days in my mind, please let it happen. Let me linger at her bedside. Let me hug a little longer. Let me sing one more song. Let me rock her long after she has fallen asleep. By Your mercy, I will remember all of these days and give You praise. Amen.

The child grew and became strong; he was filled with wisdom, and the grace of God was on him.

—Luke 2:40

Laughter and Dancing

SWEET JESUS,

Surely we are born for laughter and dancing. Our baby proves it to me. Her laugh is among the finest and purest I have ever known. She cackles aloud at the most surprising things. A simple hello can send her into a wave of silliness and giggles. The delight of her own laughter produces jitterbug feet and cha-cha arms.

Thank You that she laughs so effortlessly. May it always be so. Protect her heart and her spirit from the things that rob her joy. She is completely innocent and pure. I know that the world will come around to find her one day, but may she always remember how to laugh from her heart.

I once heard a man say that he could tell a lot about people by the way they laugh. I have come to believe the great truth of his words. Real laughter—spontaneous, readily available, and unmanufactured—can come only from a person of peace and contentment. It comes only from a person who is looking for joy.

Let her always look for joy. Let her know the good medicine of rib-splitting laughter and impromptu dancing. May she learn this fine art from her parents. Fill our home with comedy and wit, ballet and the Flat Rock Stomp, great fun and silliness. You gave us marvelous gifts when You gave us a time to laugh and a time to dance. Thank You for life's fun. Thank You for a baby who reminds us all to loosen up a little, look for the joy, and giggle. From our immense pleasure, we give You praise. Amen.

There is a time for everything, and a season for every activity under heaven…
a time to weep and a time to laugh, a time to mourn and a time to dance.

—*Ecclesiastes 3:1,4*

My Baby-in-Love

Sweet God,

What a privilege it is to pray for our baby's future mate. Imagine! Our child will one day choose someone to love and to cherish forever. And we will welcome him into our home and love him as our own.

Wherever he is, Lord, I pray that he will know great devotion and protection. Let his parents love him with a mighty love and shelter his heart from evil. I pray for a childhood that is tender, carefree, and filled with lots of play and laughter. Let somebody tell him over and over how much he is loved and valued. Give him the security of a family and place to call home.

Inspire his learning and increase his bounty of common sense. Let him come to know You as Savior at the earliest possible age. Give him wisdom in his life choices. Encourage him to choose purity and wait for the true love of our child. Show him the blessings of walking with You.

My heart is glad to pray for the other baby who will grow up and come to our family through love. Remind me to pray for him often. You know him by name, and I smile to think that someday our daughter will meet the one You have in mind for her.

Because I believe in the power of prayer, and because I want the best possible mate for our child, I will pray until I meet our "baby-in-love." May Your will be done. Because I love You, I will trust You. Amen.

*D*o not be yoked together
with unbelievers. For what do
righteousness and wickedness
have in common? Or what
fellowship can light have
with darkness?

—2 Corinthians 6:14

A wife of noble character
who can find? She is worth
far more than rubies.

—*Proverbs 31:10*

*H*usbands, love your wives,
just as Christ loved the
church and gave himself up
for her to make her holy.

—Ephesians 5:25-26

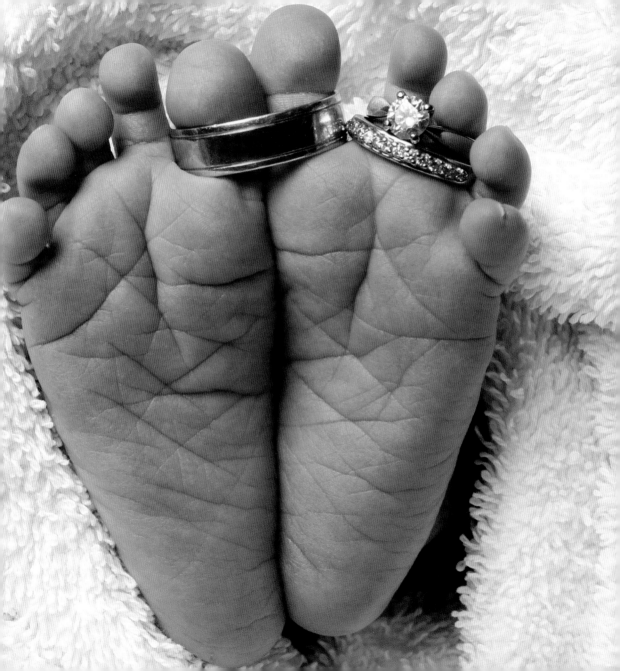

Our Sick Baby

Oh, Great Physician,

Today, our tiny angel wrestles with her first fever and infection. After a very long night, we are both worn out. It broke my heart to listen to her cry out in pain when I laid her down. She could only get comfortable enough to take little naps in my arms. So, we rocked and walked all night. Morning couldn't dawn soon enough. We had to be first in line at our pediatrician's office.

When we arrived, I quickly realized we weren't the only distressed parents in town. The line formed quickly with all the other moms and dads holding their teary-eyed, pajama-clad children. Obviously, they had also been up all night, taking temperatures and measuring ibuprofen. We were all comparing symptoms and lamenting our little ones' sickness.

Lord, thank You for the nurses and our kind pediatrician. What a welcome relief to trust my suffering daughter to these qualified professionals for diagnosis and care. Thank You that the doctor notices the concern in my eyes and speaks to my fears. Thank You for an antibiotic that will restore health.

I pray for complete healing for my sweet little girl. Nothing else seems to matter when our baby is sick. Please restore full health to her body. Remove all the infection, and give her an afternoon of good rest. Give me wisdom as I provide comfort and help. Lord, I thank You in advance for the healing You will bring. By the power of Jesus, who healed those who were in need, I pray. Amen.

The prayer offered in faith will make the sick person well.

—*James 5:15*

The crowds…followed Him; and welcoming them,
He began speaking to them about the kingdom of
God and curing those who had need of healing.

—*Luke 9:11* NASB

A Bath-Time Prayer

Dear Lord,

Bath time brings such beautiful moments with my baby. She loves the warmth of the water. Splashing is already her favorite game. A bath always pacifies and relaxes her fussy, ready-to-go-to-bed body. This nighttime ritual helps wash away the day and prepares her for a sound sleep.

As I bathe her, I pray for her body. I pray that she will continue to grow in strength and in stature. Give her strong legs to run and play and do ballet, arms that can knock a ball right out of the park, a heart that will last for a long life, keen vision, acute hearing, and the ability to speak well. Strengthen her mind so she can learn and process and develop. Protect her from injury and disease. So much goes on under that skin. I must trust that nothing goes unseen by Your watchful eye.

What a privilege it is to hold in my arms a place where You abide. What a privilege it is to hold on to a temple. Lord, I pray that, in addition to caring for her physical body, You would care for her tender little spirit as well. Protect her soul until she can choose You for her own. Shelter her mind from any harm. Guard the precious wellspring of her heart.

I commit to do all that I can to care for this one. I entrust all that I cannot do to You. When I hold my fresh-smelling baby in a big fuzzy towel, I am moved by the greatness of Your gift to me. Thank You for her. I love You. Amen.

***

*D*on't you know that you yourselves are God's temple and that God's Spirit dwells in your midst?

—1 Corinthians 3:16

Our Baby's Dedication

Precious Lord,

We come to dedicate the life of our daughter to You. We know full well that she is Your treasure. You only lend her to us for a while. We promise to take care of her and love her with all our might. We promise to teach her that You love her even more than we do. We promise to give parenting every valiant effort.

Lord, we come to this task completely dependent on You. Give us great wisdom and discernment in the decisions ahead. Temper our discipline and instruction with gentleness and grace. Help us to always consider how our actions and words may affect the Spirit of God inside her.

There is no way to predict what the years hold for our family, so we must walk each day in total surrender to Your plan and Your purpose. We take every step assuming that You have already supplied the courage and resources we'll need. We dream and hope for the future, expecting that You're already there.

We thankfully dedicate our child to her almighty God and Creator. Work in her life to Your glory. Keep her set apart and protected. From the depth of our gratitude, we praise You. Amen.

I prayed for this child, and the Lord has granted me what
I asked of him. So now I give him to the Lord. For his
whole life he will be given over to the Lord.

—1 Samuel 1:27-28

A Mother's Love

MY HEAVENLY FATHER,

I didn't know I possessed the ability to love like a mother until I had a child. With this baby, I reaffirm my love and commitment. In Your presence, I promise to:

- ❧ keep her clean and clothed and fed
- ❧ do whatever it takes to model goodness and godliness
- ❧ care greatly about her character
- ❧ discipline her
- ❧ tell her about Jesus, her Savior
- ❧ rejoice with her on the good days and hold her on the bad days
- ❧ be interruptible for the rest of my life
- ❧ read to her and sing to her and teach her to dance
- ❧ introduce her to the rest of Your creation
- ❧ praise her
- ❧ be a well of deep grace she can always come home to
- ❧ give her strong wings and a desire to fly

Mothering is a high and holy privilege. More than anything else, I want to finish well. I solemnly dedicate my entire lifetime to this great purpose. May You be pleased with my offering. By the power of Christ Jesus, I pray. Amen.

The woman whose son was alive was deeply moved out of love for her son and said to the king, "Please, my lord, give her the living baby! Don't kill him!"

But the other said, "Neither I nor you shall have him. Cut him in two!"

Then the king gave his ruling: "Give the living baby to the first woman. Do not kill him; she is his mother."

—1 Kings 3:26-27

Salvation

Jesus,

I am privileged to pray for my daughter's salvation. My prayers for her began when she was being formed in the womb. Now, I commit to continue in prayer until she believes. Luke 15:10 says there is rejoicing in the presence of angels when one sinner repents. Heaven throws a party when one person comes to know You as Savior!

If the party is in the presence of angels, then the giver of the party must be You. When the lost are found and the old become new, You declare a celestial celebration. You initiate all the hoopla. You proclaim, "Let the rejoicing begin; My child whom I love has come home." I can just imagine dancing and singing and great anthems of praise. If heaven gets excited about the salvation of one, then how can I do any less? I will gladly pray for this joyous event.

For my child I pray that she finds salvation early in her life. Please keep her from too many wasted and wandering years. I didn't know any real purpose for my life until I knew You. May she come to know You very soon.

Teach us to guide and not smother. May we offer Your gift without force. We want her decision to be her own. May she soon know the tender love of Your merciful forgiveness and the joy of Your grace. May she live all of her life sheltered by Your compassionate hand. Because You are the only way to eternal life, I pray from the power of Your sacrifice. Amen.

I tell you, there is rejoicing in the presence of the
angels of God over one sinner who repents.

—Luke 15:10

The Tablet of Her Heart

God of all wisdom,

Perhaps our greatest parenting challenge is figuring out how to write on the tablet of our daughter's heart. I mean, just how is that going to happen? Will our words be enough? Will our lives measure up to our teaching? What if we sabotage our own efforts through sin and mistakes? And how will we know that the ink with which we write is permanent ink? Won't the world try to erase all we put in there?

I pray that I might mold the soft, pliable spirit of my daughter and engrave her soul with the markings of kindness and love. My prevailing ambition is to teach her about goodness and have her embrace it as her own, to show her loyalty and watch her become loyal, to give her grace and watch as she, in turn, gives it to others, and to introduce her to my Savior and have her choose Jesus for herself.

I'm not exactly sure how this transfer will happen. I must claim the truth of Proverbs 3 for my life—I cannot lean on my own understanding. Instead, I will trust in You. In every decision I make, I will seek You. I believe You will write on the tablet of our child's heart, even those things that we, in our humanness, are not able to impart.

Sometimes, the enormity of our task scares me. Our precious child. A moldable character. Therefore, we entrust this most valuable treasure into Your hands. By Your wisdom and from Your leading, she will know righteousness all the days of her life. In Jesus' name, I pray. Amen.

---

*L*et love and faithfulness never leave you; bind them around your neck, write them on the tablet of your heart. Then you will win favor and a good name in the sight of God and man. Trust in the Lord with all your heart and lean not on your own understanding; in all your ways submit to him, and he will make your paths straight.

—Proverbs 3:3-6

Yet you brought me out of the womb;
you made me trust in you, even at my
mother's breast. From birth I was cast
on you; from my mother's womb
you have been my God.

—Psalm 22:9-10

God is able to bless you
abundantly, so that in all things
at all times, having all that you
need, you will abound in
every good work.

—2 Corinthians 9:8

The LORD bless you and
keep you; the LORD make
his face shine on you and
be gracious to you; the LORD
turn his face toward you
and give you peace.

—Numbers 6:24-26

Keepsakes

LORD,

There are so many things to cherish:

❀ a tiny ID bracelet

❀ a newborn hospital cap and booties

❀ the newspaper from the day of her birth

❀ a pink bubblegum cigar

❀ her homecoming dress

❀ two tiny ink footprints on paper

❀ a lock of hair tied with a ribbon of pink

❀ that first squinty-eyed picture

❀ the gifts our family presented

❀ a white crocheted blanket

❀ a tiny pink Bible

These are my baby's keepsakes. To look at them is precious. To touch them is to hold my newborn again. Thank You for little treasures that remind me of that wonderful day she was born. For the sake of our memories, we keep holding on to the reminders...souvenirs for our soul.

Thank You, Jesus. Amen.

Mary treasured up all these things and
pondered them in her heart.

—*Luke 2:19*

Ninety-fifth Percentile

Lord,

Our daughter's weight and height now place her in the ninety-fifth percentile on the growth charts. Certainly no two babies are exactly the same. That must be the key to this whole thing. Extra big or average-sized, they are all individuals to be loved. I must value baby's differences as much as I love her similarities.

She is exactly the person You created. She reflects the image of our family in her own distinct and unique ways. She has features like many of our family members and the same infectious smile You gave her daddy. She definitely belongs with our tribe, but lately she's been showing us that she's more different than she's the same.

I must accept the fact that, even though we are mother and daughter, we will surely be different in many ways. Her future is not mine to live. I cannot force her to share my interests. I risk the chance of wounding her spirit. I want to look for her gifts and nurture them. I want to see her uniqueness and applaud it. I want to be the mother and let her be the daughter.

Lord, You knew our daughter before You formed her. You have set her apart for a special work. May we bless her as our daughter and give her the freedom to be the person You intend for her to be. By Your grace, she will always remain distinctly Yours. Amen.

Before I formed you in the womb I knew you, before you were born I set you apart.

—Jeremiah 1:5

The Blessing

Lord,

Bless our sweet darling. Hold her securely in Your strong hands of mercy. Protect her. Defend her. Send a myriad of angels to guard every step she takes. Strengthen her body. Keep sickness away. We entrust our priceless treasure to You for safekeeping.

May she come to know You intimately as her personal Savior. May she always find rest in Your great arms of love. May Your awesome works as Almighty God overwhelm her. May she abide always in her Redeemer's arms of grace. May she serve You as Lord. May she trust You as Friend. Give her an unswerving faith and an unquenchable thirst for You this side of heaven.

Let her grow in great wisdom and honor. Give her an inquisitive mind and a hunger for knowledge. Endow her with common sense and the ability to apply all that her mind possesses. Give her an unfailing sense of what is right. May she be a woman of integrity. A woman of principle. A woman of purity. Honest. Diligent. Compelling. Generous. Kind. Good. May she be a virtuous woman of God.

Give her a wonderful family; a marvelous man to love and adore for a lifetime and children who will rise up and call her blessed. Allow her enough struggles to grow character. Bestow on her the rewards of perseverance. May she preserve the legacy of our family and pursue holiness all the days of her life.

We invoke Your blessing for this precious baby in the name of the Father, the Son, and the Holy Spirit. May You receive all the glory and honor both now and forever. Amen.